Out There?

MYSTERIES OF THE DEEP

John Townsend

Raintree

Chicago, Illinois

For information, address the publisher:
Raintree, 100 N. LaSalle, Suite 1200, Chicago, IL 60602
Printed and bound in China
08 07 06 05 04
10 9 8 7 6 5 4 3 2 1

Library of Congress Cataloging-in-Publication Data
Townsend, John, 1955-
  Mysteries of the deep / John Townsend.
     v. cm. -- (Out there?)
Includes bibliographical references and index.
Contents: Mystery through time -- Lost below the waves -- Mystery ships
-- Disaster -- Mystery powers -- Secret life -- Mystery to knowledge.
  ISBN 1-4109-0562-4 (lib. bdg.), 1-4109-0963-8 (Pbk.)
  1. Curiosities and wonders--Juvenile literature. 2. Sea stories. [1.
Curiosities and wonders. 2. Sea stories.] I. Title.
  G557.T68 2004
  910'.02162--dc21
                          2003010542

Acknowledgments
The author and publishers would like to thank the following for permission to reproduce copyright materials: Pp. 4–5, 32–33, 44, 45, 46 NHPA; pp. 5 (top), 8–9, 16–17 Robert Harding; pp. 5 (middle), 6, 9, 11, 12, 14, 17, 19, 20, 20–21, 22–23, 26, 26–27, 27, 28–29, 29, 32, 33, 34–35, 35, 36, 37, 42, 48, 48–49, 49, 50 Corbis; pp. 5 (bottom), 38–39 Agence Nature/NHPA; pp. 6–7 Topham Picturepoint; p. 7 Getty Images; pp. 8, 14–15, 23, 30, 50–51 Photodisc; pp. 10–11 Wm Leo Smith; pp. 12–13, 14–15, 21, 24, 31 Mary Evans Picture Library; p. 13 Wade Pemberton; p. 15 Ancient Egypt Picture Library; pp. 18–19 Photo Library Ltd./Corbis; p. 22 Hulton Archives; pp. 24–25, 42–43, 47 Ronald Grant Archives; pp. 36–37, 44–45 Pete Atkinson/NHPA; p. 38 Kim Reisenbichler/Monterey Bay Aquarium Research Institute; pp. 38–39 Norbert Wu/NHPA; pp. 40, 40–41, 41 A.N.T./NHPA; p. 43 Nature Picture Library.

Cover photograph used with permission of: FLPA/D. Fleetham/Silvestris/Still Pictures.

CONTENTS

Some words are shown in bold, **like this.** You can find out what they mean by looking in the glossary. You can also look out for them in the "Weird Words" box at the bottom of each page.

THE GREAT UNKNOWN

The oceans of the world are full of secrets. Will we ever know what is hidden in their depths? Underwater mountains, canyons, and caves could hide another world. Scientists think there are millions of creatures that they do not yet know about in the mud at the bottom of the oceans.

THE DEEPEST WATERS

This table shows the earth's deepest bodies of water.

There are even deeper **trenches** and underwater caves that no one has explored.

SECRET WORLD

From the time people first set sail in ships, they had to cope with the great power of the sea. Sailors told stories of its magic, its monsters, and its mystery. But even now it is hard to imagine the real size of the oceans. The Pacific Ocean alone holds half the world's water. It holds thousands of lost ships, too.

OCEANS	DEEPEST PARTS
Pacific Ocean	6.8 mi (11 km)
Atlantic Ocean	5.7 mi (9 km)
Indian Ocean	4.6 mi (7.5 km)
Caribbean Sea	4.3 mi (7 m)
Arctic Ocean	3.5 mi (5.5 m)

lurk wait around, ready to strike
seabed floor at the bottom of the ocean or sea

DEEP BLUE SEA

Seventy percent of the earth is made up of water. Some of it is as deep as twenty-eight Empire State buildings standing on top of each other. It can be so cold and dark in places that no one has ever been down to the bottom. In fact, more people have been up in outer space than down into the deepest ocean. The pressure of the water would crush you to death in seconds. But now, cameras and special submarines can dive very deep to show us what hides on the **seabed.**

The 21st century will be a time of discovery as we start to explore more mysteries of the deep.

A blue whale is so huge that a soccer team could stand on its tongue!

FIND OUT LATER . . .

Do secrets still lie in the wrecks at the bottom of the sea?

Are there really great powers locked in the oceans?

*What kinds of creatures **lurk** in the depths of the ocean?*

trench deep ditch, gully, or valley

MYSTERY THROUGH TIME

SEA GODS

The Romans believed Neptune was the god who ruled the oceans. If they upset him, their ship would sink. The Greeks had to please a god named Poseidon. The sea's storms and scary creatures were all thought to be controlled by the gods.

The seas have always terrified people who have had to sail in its storms. Sailors in ancient Greece used to believe they had to please the gods to make the oceans stay calm. Even today there are many **superstitions** about the seas.

THE KRAKEN

Myths and storytelling over hundreds of years have added to the sea's mystery. Tales such as that of the kraken from Norway still amaze us. The **Vikings** were early sailors who told of a huge sea monster called the kraken that looked like a giant octopus. The kraken could sink any ship and eat everyone on board. The kraken could even suck a whole ship down into the sea.

OLD IDEAS

When sailors thought the world was flat, they were in constant fear of falling off the edge of the earth. They thought that if they sailed too far, they would reach the land of the devil. Or maybe they would meet Neptune, the god of the sea. Meeting Neptune was thought to bring certain death. And where did Neptune live? In the Sargasso Sea. That is in the middle of the Bermuda Triangle, a place still known for its danger.

Many Roman statues show Neptune, god of the sea. **‹‹**

WEIRD WORDS

myth   made-up tale, told over many years
omen   sign that may bring good or evil

BAD LUCK

Sailors often felt they were in danger and needed luck. But many things were thought to bring bad luck. If a cross-eyed woman looked at a ship, it was believed she would bring disaster.

Cats were kept on ships to kill rats and bring luck.

BELIEFS

The ship's cat could be an **omen.** Black cats have always been linked with luck. But they were said to bring storms if they cleaned their paws within sight of a ship. If a live rabbit ever went on board, the ship was doomed.

Pictures of the kraken have been drawn from sailors' stories.

superstition belief based on faith in the supernatural
Vikings Scandinavian sailors from long ago

THE FAMOUS MERMAID

The Little Mermaid of Copenhagen is Denmark's most famous statue. The Danish writer Hans Christian Andersen told the story of the daughter of the Sea King. She lived in the deepest sea, "where the sea people live." The story says that she saved a prince from drowning.

MYTH AND LEGEND

Sailors have told tales of strange sea creatures that have puzzled the world for years. But are these stories from sailors' imaginations, or even tricks of the mind? Many sailors swear they have really seen **mermaids** in the ocean.

MERMAIDS

Mermaids have been part of sailors' **folklore** for centuries. Can there really be creatures in the ocean with the head and body of a human and the tail of a large fish? There have been many reports of mermaids from all around the world for hundreds of years. Sailors used to dread seeing a mermaid, since it was a sure sign that their ship would run into trouble.

mermaid mythical sea creature with the body of a beautiful woman and the tail of a fish

ALIVE AND WELL?

For years, people have reported seeing mermaids off the coast of Hawaii. In 1998 someone claimed to have taken a photo of the Kaiwi Point Mermaid. He said, "She had long, flowing hair and one of the most beautiful faces I've ever seen." So even today some people believe mermaids really exist.

SIRENS

A **siren** was a beautiful creature that was half woman and half bird. She was said to sing so sweetly that sailors would go into a **trance**. They would dive into the sea to be with her and then they would drown. Or the siren's singing would make sailors steer their ship into the deadly rocks.

THE MANATEE

Anyone seeing a manatee for the first time would be puzzled. These large, gentle mammals are gray with pink patches on their skin. Perhaps from a distance they look like mermaids?

Maybe sailors mistook seals, dolphins, or manatees for mermaids.

siren beautiful female creature in Greek myths whose singing would attract sailors and then bring disaster

SERPENTS OF THE DEEP

Some books describe a monster as "an animal of strange or terrifying shape and very large for its kind." In that case, the ocean is home to some real monsters. But we are still not certain whether giant sea serpents exist.

FEAR OF THE UNKNOWN

Before people knew about some of the world's real sea creatures, they must have been scared whenever a fin or tail splashed to the surface of the water. It is easy to see why sailors believed in weird beasts. Even today, there are reports of USOs, as some sailors call them. These are Unidentified Swimming Objects—like **UFOs** that appear in the oceans.

SNAKE OF THE SEA

The most common USO reported over the years is a giant sea **serpent**. Many reports describe huge, dark sea snakes 160 feet (50 meters) long. Some have a seaweed-like **mane** and fierce, staring eyes. They could still be out there.

mane long hair growing on the neck

CLOSE ENCOUNTER

A ship called the *Hilary* was sailing near Iceland in 1917. A creature with a head like a cow and a body 66 feet (20 meters) long suddenly rose from the sea. The sailors shot at it, and the creature sank without a trace. They never knew if they hit it or if it dived back into the water.

THE OARFISH

Could an oarfish be mistaken for a sea serpent? It is one of the strangest-looking fish. It has a silver body and a bright red mane that runs down its back. Oarfish live in deep seas and only come up to the surface when they are sick.

Some oarfish grow to be 66 ft (20 m) long.

SERPENTS OR GIANT EELS?

- In Roman times, emperors threw criminals into tanks of large, hungry eels.
- Tales of "monster" human-eating eels go back many years.
- A 6.6-ft (2-m) baby eel was found in 1930. It could have grown into an adult that would have been about 98 ft (30 m) long. No more have been found.

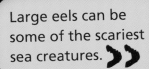

Large eels can be some of the scariest sea creatures.

serpent large snake
UFO Unidentified Flying Object

11

LOST BELOW THE WAVES

THE SARGASSO SEA

The Sargasso Sea near the island of Bermuda has thick seaweed. Eels come here from all over the world to **spawn**. The rich seaweed protects their eggs. Why does so much of it grow here? Some say it is fed by Atlantis deep below.

There are many stories about a rich land full of gold and jewels. It was a fine city that was at the center of a great **continent** until it sank forever. It is believed the city is now deep beneath the ocean. Many people have tried to find it. The Greek writer Plato first wrote about the lost land of Atlantis in 350 B.C.E.

ATLANTIS

Why did the sea drown Atlantis? Did sea levels suddenly rise? Was there an **earthquake** or a giant wave? Many **legends** describe a great flood about 11,000 years ago, when **volcanoes** and storms hit Earth. Maybe the water rose too high and drowned Atlantis.

Feeding on the lost world? Parts of the Sargasso Sea are 4.4 miles (7 kilometers) deep. **‹‹**

continent one of the earth's seven large land masses
fate power thought to control what will happen

WHERE?

Atlantis remains one of the sea's great mysteries. Of all the world's unsolved puzzles, the **fate** of Atlantis is especially strange. Apart from the question "Did Atlantis really exist?," we want to know where it was. And where is it now?

Some people say the lost land is now far below the ice of Antarctica. Others believe it is in the middle of the Indian Ocean. But the mysterious Sargasso Sea around Bermuda may hold more secrets. This is the area of the Bermuda Triangle, where many boats have gone missing. Perhaps Atlantis lies at the bottom of the Sargasso Sea. With the area's strange mists and thick seaweed, Atlantis will stay hidden forever.

Is this part of a lost world under the sea?

THE ROAD TO ATLANTIS

Near the Sargasso Sea, there is a strange line of stones a fifth of a mile (one-third km) long beneath the sea. This pathway was found in 1968 near the Bimini Islands. Some say it is just a **rock formation,** but others think this "Bimini Road" leads to Atlantis.

A painting of what Atlantis may have looked like. **❮❮**

rock formation natural feature made by the wearing away or movement of rock
spawn lay many eggs

Melting glaciers are raising the sea level all the time. ⌄⌄

SINKING

Many lands have vanished beneath the sea. Some old maps of the Pacific Ocean show islands that no longer exist. **Earthquakes** can make land fall into the ocean. But more often, the sea rises slowly, foot by foot, as ice at the poles melts. Towns and countryside could be lost forever.

SUNK

The land of Lemuria was said to be the Garden of Eden, where the human race began. Now it is thought to lie below the Indian Ocean. Another land called Mu may have been drowned by the Pacific Ocean. Its story was told on ancient **stone tablets** that were hidden in a **Hindu** temple.

THE END OF AN AGE

Many islands were doomed when warmer weather ended the **Ice Age.** Melting ice fell into the ocean and the water level rose. In many places, it has been rising ever since. Many towns by the sea have been destroyed. Old Dunwich, in Great Britain, fell into the sea. Some say its church bells still clang below the waves.

Divers hope to find lost treasure. ⌄⌄

Hindu belonging to the ancient Indian religion of Hinduism. It is still practiced today.

ALEXANDRIA, EGYPT

The Lighthouse of Alexandria was a beautiful tower built above the Egyptian rocks for all to see. It guided sailors for sixteen centuries. It saved many from drowning, but it could not save itself. It crashed into the sea hundreds of years ago when an earthquake struck. Part of the city of Alexandria fell into the ocean with the lighthouse.

FOUND

In 1934 a huge marble head from a statue of Alexander the Great was lifted from the water. Alexander was the famous leader who built the city. Local fishermen had known about its lost buildings for years. They used to swim through the underwater ruins.

PORT ROYAL, JAMAICA

Just before noon on June 7, 1692, an earthquake hit the West Indies. Much of Kingston Harbor in Jamaica fell into the sea. About 2,000 people were killed instantly. Divers have since found shops and restaurants in the underwater streets.

A marble statue from Alexandria has been rescued from the **seabed.** ««

Ice Age when much of the Earth was covered with ice
stone tablets slabs of stone that are carved with writing

AUSTRALIA'S SHIPWRECK COAST

Hundreds of wrecks lie in the sands off the coast of Victoria, Australia. Ships full of silver or spices met their end on the rocks in storms. The first was the *Tryall* in 1622. Since then, more than 700 ships have been lost along this rocky coast.

GOLD AND SILVER

Many people love to hear stories of sunken treasure. The **seabed** could be hiding many treasure chests packed with fine things. Ships used to carry all kinds of riches. There are thousands of wrecks in the oceans, and many have never been found.

FLORIDA

Off the coast of Florida is a ships' graveyard. Storms here have smashed many boats against the **reefs** over the years. In 1715 ten Spanish ships sank in one night. In addition to tobacco and sugar, they were carrying treasure. An eleventh ship, the *Urca de Lima*, **survived** the storm. But it sank in the next night's storm and lost all its gold and silver coins.

Scuba divers can explore the wrecks off the Australian coast.

dreaded feared
fleet large group of ships

VICTIMS OF THE ANGRY SEA

In July 1733 another Spanish **fleet** of treasure ships came to a watery end off the Florida coast. More than twenty ships were full of treasures from the Americas. The ships were taking gold and spices back to Spain. They had just left Cuba when the storm struck a **dreaded** area of sea that is famous for hurricanes. Today it is called the Bermuda Triangle.

Before they could get to shelter, the ships were smashed by giant waves. Only one ship escaped. The others were scattered and wrecked along the Upper Florida Keys. The wrecks stayed there for over 200 years. Modern-day treasure hunters have now taken everything valuable.

►►►►►►►►►►

Find out more about the Bermuda Triangle on page 30.

FULL-TIME TREASURE HUNTER

Robert Ballard's job is finding sunken ships. He has found ships in the Black Sea that are over 1,500 years old. He also looks for clues about great floods, like those of Noah's Ark and maybe Atlantis.

Robert Ballard (center) has discovered some of the oldest shipwrecks, including the *Titanic*.

reef ridge of rock or coral near the surface of the sea

MYSTERY SHIPS

GUARD AGAINST GHOST SHIPS

There were many **superstitions** that sailors thought would help keep their ships safe.

Sailors had a lot to be afraid of, including sea creatures, storms, and dangerous rocks. Yet ocean journeys could be calm and usually took many days. Sounds and shapes in the mist would stir sailors' imaginations.

LOOK OUT!

Each ship was said to have a soul. Sailors believed that if a ship sank, its soul would keep sailing the seas. That is how sailors explained some of the ghostly shapes they saw in the fog. But if they met a ghost ship, it was bad news. It meant the sailors were doomed and they would never see land again.

To pass the time, sailors often told mysterious stories.

Nail horseshoes to ships' masts for protection.

Break a bottle to launch a ship. This is an offering to the gods for protection.

Do not carry a black bag onto a ship. It is bad luck.

WEIRD WORDS

curse words that bring about supernatural powers
legend story from long ago that may be partly true

THE *FLYING DUTCHMAN*

An old sea **legend** told of a Dutch sea captain whose ship, the *Flying Dutchman*, met a storm off the coast of South Africa. The Cape of Good Hope is famous for its stormy seas, and the captain feared he would drown. He screamed a **curse**, "I WILL get around this Cape even if I have to sail forever!"

THE CURSE

Ever since, sailors say they have seen the *Flying Dutchman* adrift in storms. It was meant to be bad luck for anyone who saw the ghost ship. No sailor would sail on any ship that had met the *Flying Dutchman*. It became a curse of the seas.

THE CAPE OF GOOD HOPE

The Cape of Good Hope is at the southern tip of Africa. Winds and high waves meet here with great force. It was once called the Cape of Storms. Many ships have met a violent end here, and sailors **dread** these waters.

The sea off the coast of South Africa can be deadly in a storm, even for modern boats.

soul spirit of a person or place that is said to last forever

THE FREEZING SEA

Old sailing ships in Arctic waters faced dangers other than icebergs. Their masts and decks would clog up with ice and snow. This would make them top-heavy. **Whaling ships** were often wrecked in icy storms around Baffin Island in the North Atlantic.

GHOSTLY TALE

Mystery surrounds a ship called the *Rescue*. In 1860 it met another American ship in a storm near Baffin Island in the North Atlantic. The *Rescue* was in great danger, so the crew climbed aboard the larger ship, the *George Henry,* just in time. By the next day, the *Rescue* had vanished.

A year later the *George Henry* was back near Baffin Island, and its sailors reported a strange sight. From out of the icy mist, the *Rescue* appeared again. Its decks were full of snow as it creaked and drifted through the icebergs.

Sailors say the icy ship still haunts the North Atlantic today.

Massive icebergs can easily wreck ships.

PHANTOM SAILOR

Joseph Slocum was famous for being the first man to sail alone around the world. It took him three years. He left Boston in 1895 in his boat the *Spray*. A storm blew for days, and Joseph fought to keep his boat from sinking. Worn out, he fell asleep. When he woke up, the *Spray* was gliding through huge waves. On deck he saw an old sailor steering the boat. Joseph was sure a ghost had come to save him.

In 1909 Joseph set sail from Massachusetts for South America. He was 65 when he left, and he was never seen again. No one knows what happened to him.

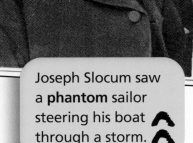

Joseph Slocum saw a **phantom** sailor steering his boat through a storm.

WHO WAS THE SHADOWY FIGURE?

The mysterious figure wore clothes from the 1400s and said he was from the *Pinta*. That was one of Christopher Columbus's ships that sailed in 1492 to find the **New World**.

phantom ghostly appearance
whaling ship ship used for hunting whales

THE U-65 SUBMARINE MYSTERY

How could one submarine have so much back luck?:

* On the first sea trial, the engine room filled with fumes and killed three men.

* In calm waters, a man fell overboard and was lost.

* Just after a priest tried to get rid of the jinx, a gunner went crazy and an engineer broke his leg.

THE HAUNTED U-BOAT

Even before the German submarine U-65 sailed in World War I, it had bad luck. An officer was one of ten men killed when a **torpedo** exploded while they were loading it. Soon afterward sailors saw the officer's ghost standing on deck. Then the submarine captain was killed during a battle. What else could happen to this **jinxed** submarine?

More accidents happened to men on the submarine. None could be explained. Then, in 1918, a U.S. submarine saw the U-65. Before the American captain could take aim, he saw a lone figure standing on the U-65's deck. Suddenly, the jinxed German U-boat mysteriously exploded and sank.

This German submarine was doomed.

jinx unlucky force
retire leave active service

THE HAUNTED AIRCRAFT CARRIER

In July 1967, the aircraft carrier USS *Forrestal* was off the coast of Vietnam. A Phantom Jet fighter plane on deck let off a rocket by mistake. The rocket hit the fuel tank of another jet. Suddenly, the whole deck was covered in flames. Fuel tanks and bombs exploded, and many men were blown overboard. Others were trapped below deck and burned to death. More than 130 men lost their lives, and the ship needed massive repairs.

After that, strange things happened on board the *Forrestal* before it was **retired** in 1993. Voices, doors opening, "ghostly hands," and flickering lights led people to believe a ghost was on board. They called the ghost George.

The USS *Forrestal* was 1,000 ft (300 m) long, with 19 levels.

THE USS FORRESTAL

The USS *Forrestal* was big enough to hide a ghost. It was said that George often touched sailors and even gripped one for a while. A man reported that an unused phone kept ringing. He answered it and heard a cry for help.

torpedo cigar-shaped underwater missile

DISASTER

UNSINKABLE

The *Titanic*'s owners said the ship was so safe that it did not need many lifeboats. The chances of the ship sinking were said to be one in a million. Yet 23 passengers canceled their tickets and told others they thought the ship was doomed.

Many mysteries surround the **maiden voyage** of the *Titanic*. It sank to the icy depths of the North Atlantic at 2:20 A.M. on April 15, 1912. In total, 1,513 men, women, and children were lost. The world was stunned by the news. How could this happen when it had been built to be unsinkable?

STRANGE PASSENGER

One mystery was why William Stead was on board. A number of people reported his story afterward. He had made a fuss about the number of lifeboats on the *Titanic*. He did not think there were enough. He turned out to be right, but he still set sail.

WHITE STAR LINE

Titanic Facts

Total **capacity**: 3,320 people
Number of lifeboats: 20
Lifeboat capacity: 1,178 people
Top Speed: 25 knots (29 mph)
Passengers onboard: 2,224
Number of **survivors**: 705

These *Titanic* postcards were never used. **‹‹**

I.T.S.S.TITANIC.

WEIRD WORDS   **capacity** number of people that can fit on board
maiden voyage first journey of a ship

WARNINGS

A **psychic** had warned Stead not to sail on the *Titanic*. He had other warnings from strangers. One woman told him he would "soon be called home." It was later said that as the *Titanic* sailed out of Southampton, Great Britain, a woman in the crowd cried, "That ship is going to sink! Do something! Save them!"

TRAGEDY

Four days later, the great ship hit an iceberg. There were too few lifeboats to save all of the 2,224 passengers and crew. William Stead was among the 1,513 people who died. It is not hard to imagine what his last thoughts must have been as the ship went down.

The *Titanic* was the world's largest oceanliner. ❱❱

JUST LIKE THE *TITANIC*...

In 1898, fourteen years before the *Titanic* sank, Morgan Robertson wrote a book about a ship named the *Titan*. In the story, *Titan*

- was British and sailed in April;
- had a top speed of 25 knots;
- had just over 2,000 passengers;
- hit an iceberg and sank with many lives lost.

psychic someone able to see the future and show unusual powers of the mind

FAMOUS LAST WORDS

The *Titanic's* captain believed the ship was unsinkable.

I cannot imagine an event that would cause a ship to **flounder**. Modern ship building has gone beyond that.

E.J. Smith, Titanic Captain

THE WRECK OF THE *TITANIC*

For years it was a big mystery. Just where was the wreck of the *Titanic*?

It took over seventy years to find the wreck. Experts knew roughly where it was, but for years it was too far down for divers to reach. At last, **sonar** images showed solid shapes on the **seabed**. The scientist and diver Robert Ballard and his team found the *Titanic* in 1985. They had been searching for five years. The submarine dives helped show how the *Titanic* sank. The ship had gone down fast. It had split in two as it sank. The wreck lies in two parts, torn between the third and fourth **funnels**.

This photo of the first-class area was taken just before the *Titanic* sailed.

flounder struggle to stay afloat
funnel large, metal chimney

SILENT WORLD

Cameras and small subs have filmed the wreck lying in feet of mud. The anchors, rails, and funnels are all still there. A lamp from the grand staircase is still in one piece. There is now **coral** growing out of it.

All human remains are gone. The water and mud on the seabed contained enough acid to destroy bodies and bones over time. Robert Ballard made seven dives before leaving a **plaque** in memory of those who lost their lives that night in 1912.

The wreck of the *Titanic* is now left alone as a lasting grave to the hundreds of people who died.

The *Titanic* rests just off the coast of Newfoundland, almost 2.5 mi (4 km) deep.

MYSTERIES

Many **rumors** said something else sank the *Titanic*

- A crashed spaceship was said to lie near the wreck.
- An Egyptian mummy was said to be in the hold, being taken to a museum in New York. Did the mummy's **curse** sink the ship?

This cherub statue from the famous staircase has been brought up from the shipwreck.

plaque stone or metal sign in memory of the dead
sonar use of sound waves to detect objects underwater

THE SHIP'S CAT

THE MYSTERY OF THE *JOYITA*

A 76 foot- (23-meter) long fishing boat called the *Joyita* left an island in the Pacific in 1955. It had 25 people on board. The boat was made with cork to stop it from sinking. The pleasure trip to the Tokelau Islands should have taken 48 hours, but the *Joyita* never arrived. Five weeks later a passing ship near Fiji spotted the *Joyita* 600 miles (966 kilometers) off course. It was adrift and deserted and the ship's **logbook** was missing. On deck there were blood-stained bandages. No trace of any of the passengers has ever been found. The *Joyita* is yet another mystery that is unlikely to be solved.

A cat lived on board the *Joyita*. It was seen on deck on the day the boat left on its last doomed voyage. The cat was jumpy. It ran along the deck then dashed down the plank onto dry land and disappeared. Could this have been an **omen**?

The mystery of the *Kursk* is still being investigated.

logbook official diary of a ship's voyage

THE MYSTERY OF THE KURSK

In August 2000 the world waited in fear when the Russian **nuclear submarine** *Kursk* sank. It could not rise up from the bed of the Barents Sea. A total of 118 men were stuck inside, 328 feet (100 meters) down. This was a six-year-old submarine with all the latest equipment. How could this happen?

MYSTERY EXPLOSIONS

Two explosions sent the submarine into the mud under the sea. The water down there was only 37 °F (3 °C). Inside the *Kursk*, power was out so it was pitch black. Rescue teams rushed to the scene to try to help, but it was hopeless. The *Kursk* could not be rescued, and all the men on board died.

FOUND

One of the bodies found in the *Kursk* held a note that told how 23 men remained alive after the explosions killed most of the crew. It said, "None of us can get to the surface. I am writing blindly." They were the last words he wrote.

Families of the sailors on the *Kursk* throw ❱ flowers into the sea. ❱

nuclear submarine submarine powered by nuclear (atomic) power and carrying nuclear missiles

29

MYSTERY POWERS

THE NORTH WALL

The Gulf Stream is a current of warm water that runs along the East Coast of the United States. It meets the cold Atlantic near Bermuda. The North Wall" is where the two areas of water meet. It can cause strange weather and freak waves. Maybe these waves wipe out small boats.

There are strange parts of the sea called Devil's Triangles. These are places where ships and planes often are lost. Islands lie at the three points of the triangles. The most famous is the Bermuda Triangle. Between Florida, Bermuda, and Puerto Rico is the eerie Sargasso Sea. Hundreds of people have vanished here in the last fifty years. It can be deathly still, with thick seaweed and yellow mists. Or, in sudden storms, the water can whip up and form huge waves. Planes have fallen from the sky inside the Bermuda Triangle. Radios and compasses have stopped working. Are there strange powers at work? Or is it all just **myth** and unlucky **coincidence**?

The Bermuda sea looks harmless . . . but mysteries lurk out there.

coincidence two or more seemingly connected strange things that happen at the same time

MISSING SHIPS

Small boats disappear there each year. Maybe that is not surprising, since the sea can be so stormy. But what about large ships vanishing? In 1980 a 13,200-ton cargo ship called the *Poet* disappeared with 34 people on board. The ship had just passed all its safety checks. The last anyone heard of the *Poet* was when one of the crew called his wife on the ship-to-shore radio. He told her that all was well. The ship was at the edge of the Sargasso Sea and the weather was fine. Yet the *Poet* vanished soon after this and nothing was ever found. Such mysteries just cannot be explained.

Many stories have been written about the Bermuda Triangle.

CHOPPY SEAS

Scientists can track tropical storms on radar to warn sailors about dangerous waters. But some storms can appear suddenly and destroy a boat quickly. The storms die down again before they show up on radar. Wreckage is not often found, which is another mystery.

GAS

One idea to explain why some boats vanish is that gas bubbles up from the seabed. This gas may make patches of fizzy water that stop anything from floating across. If a boat sails into a patch of gassy water like this, it will probably sink like a stone.

HOT ROCKS

Perhaps some of the things people notice at sea can be explained by nature. In some of the deep **trenches** under the ocean there are hot springs. **Vents** deep down on the **seabed** let out gas and fire. Smoking rocks **belch** out thick clouds of black smoke that rise up into the water. These smoke clouds can appear 6 miles (4 kilometers) under the water. They are very hot, but when they reach the surface, they usually just give out a puff of steam. No one on the ocean would know about the fires deep down below.

Volcanoes at sea cause many strange effects.

An underwater vent may cause ships to sink.

WEIRD WORDS erupt burst out suddenly
lava hot liquid rock that flows from a volcano

BOILING SEA

It is only in the last few years that scientists have been able to go deep to study **lava** flows on the ocean floor. Metals like copper and gold ooze up from the seabed and dissolve in the heat. Water jets from **volcanic** vents get hotter than 662 °F (350 °C). Now and again a sudden burst of gas and fire shoots up from the seabed.

If it hits the surface with a roar, a small boat could easily disappear. Could this explain why some boats vanish in parts of the Pacific Ocean? Underwater **volcanoes** often erupt in an area called the Pacific Ring of Fire.

SOME LIKE IT HOT

Is there really life down there among the gas and fire? Amazingly, yes. Tubeworms live around the vents in piping hot water. They make tasty snacks for crabs. These creatures were first found in 1977.

We have recently discovered tubeworms. What else could be **lurking** down there?

vent hole that lets out gas and smoke, like a chimney
volcano opening in the earth that lava and gas flow from

TSUNAMIS

If a large wave sweeps in from the ocean, it can be bad news. In earthquake areas this can happen a lot. The sea around Japan has many of these freak waves. They are called tsunamis.

Tsunamis are caused by earthquakes, landslides, or **volcanic eruptions** at sea.

MAKING A SPLASH

The **earth's crust** is thin in places, with many deep cracks. This is where earthquakes can happen. **Tremors** often lead to underwater **landslides** that shake up the sea. Big waves will then spread out from the middle of the **seaquake.** If the **seabed** twists and bends, the water above will swirl and splash. The ocean floor can force great amounts of water upward. This is enough to make a huge wave, like a moving wall of water. These waves are bad news for boats and bad news for people on the coast. Some of these 100-foot- (30-meter-) high waves have crashed over land and killed hundreds of people.

Earth's crust layer of rock around the earth
landslide rapid falling of earth or rocks down a slope

Date	Place	Cause and size	Deaths
February 1996	Biak, Irian Jaya	Earthquake. Waves 15–30 ft (4.5–9 m) high.	161
February 21, 1996	North coast of Peru	Earthquake. Waves 16 ft (5 m) high.	12
November 17, 1996	Near Brownsville, Texas	Bad weather. Waves 10 ft (3 m) high.	10
July 17, 1998	Papua New Guinea	Earthquake. Waves 23–49 ft (7–15 m) high.	3,000
September 15, 1999	Fatu Hiva, Marquesas Islands	Landslide. Two waves 16 ft (5 m) high.	No human lives lost

This table lists the most recent tsunamis. ◀◀

MAKING WAVES

In the open sea, a massive wave can move faster than 100 miles (160 kilometers) per hour. It slows down as it reaches the shore, but it is still fast if you are running away up the beach.

These "killer waves" are called **tsunamis,** from the Japanese *tsu* ("port") and *nami* ("wave"). They have killed thousands of people over the years. Approximately 60,000 people were killed in Portugal in 1755 by a giant wave. No one knew what caused tsunamis then. Once again people blamed the gods.

If a **meteorite** hits the ocean, it will send a giant wave toward land. Scientists think this has happened in the past. The bigger the meteorite, the bigger the wave. Who knows when the next one will strike?

A tsunami in 1992 in South America wrecked towns and killed 170 people.

meteorite large lump of rock, metal, or ice from outer space
tremor shaking caused by an earthquake

WATERSPOUTS

A **waterspout** is a tornado that moves over the ocean. It is like a whirlpool in the sky, sucking up water. It only lasts for 15 to 20 minutes. At 33–328 feet (10–100 meters) high, it spins at 66–263 feet (20–80 meters) per second. It could give a small boat a very hard time.

WHIRLPOOLS

When you pull out the bath plug you will see a mini **whirlpool** as the water swirls away. The same thing happens if an earthquake cracks a hole in the **seabed** and the sea pours down. Could some missing ships have been sucked down by a giant whirlpool? Such things may happen in the Bermuda Triangle.

GIANT SWIRLS

Strong currents and **tides** can also make whirlpools. There is a lot of mystery and **myth** surrounding them. Old Sow is the name of a whirlpool in New Brunswick, Canada. Water swirls into the bay at Deer Island Point. Strong currents meet in underwater **trenches** and stir the water into a **vortex.**

tide daily rise and fall of the oceans
vortex mass of whirling fluid in a spiral

GREAT DANGER

Before the days of motorboats, Old Sow used to swallow up boats that could not get away. In 1835 two brothers sailed from Deer Island. Their mother watched in horror from the shore as their boat was sucked down. The men were never seen again.

THE MAELSTROM

In Arctic Norway there are two great whirlpools. They form something called the Maelstrom. Four times a day the **tides** rush over a narrow ledge of rock that spikes upward from the seabed. The deep currents smash against the rock and meet surface water that is going even faster. This creates an area of rough water that grinds up any ship that goes near it.

FIVE FAMOUS AND DEADLY WHIRLPOOLS

Some of the world's largest whirlpools include:
* The Corryvreckan, North Sea, Scotland. It is a fifth of a mile (one-third km) across.
* The Old Sow, New Brunswick.
* Naruto Whirlpool, Japan. This can be viewed from a highway bridge.
* The Saltstraumen, Norway.
* The Maelstrom, Norway.

Whirlpools swirl under Naruto Bridge in Japan. **>>**

waterspout twisting column of water and spray, like a tornado over the sea

SECRET LIFE

SCARY

The vampire squid is just a few inches long, but it has the largest eyeballs of any animal. It has winglike fins and can turn tiny lights on and off all over its body. These help it to find **prey** in the dark ocean at depths of several miles.

Some of the biggest mysteries of our planet take place deep under the water. There are many undiscovered creatures down there in **trenches** and caves. Others have only been **glimpsed.** These creatures cannot **survive** at the surface. We need special deep-sea submarines and robot cameras to see them. We are only just beginning to explore the deepest corners of the oceans. Most fish in the deep ocean are blind. It is so dark that they do not need to see. Some of them are able to make their own light and glow. They have to **adapt** to great pressure and cold, too. It is a very **hostile** world down there.

The vampire squid's arms are covered with sharp spikes.

WEIRD WORDS   adapt change or adjust to new surroundings
glimpse take a quick look

STILL UNKNOWN

So far, scientists have recorded over 25,000 **species** of fish, and they think the oceans may hold another ten million species! That is more species than are known to live on land.

LIVING DINOSAUR

For years, scientists knew about a **fossil** fish. The last coelacanth (pronounced *see-la-kanth*) was thought to have died out 80 million years ago. It was a large, human-sized fish. Then, in 1938, someone caught a live one. He said it was like "finding a live dinosaur roaming the earth." More have been found since. In 1997 a scientist saw one in a fish market in Indonesia. The biggest so far weighed about 210 pounds (95 kilograms) and was about 6 feet (1.8 meters) long.

LITTLE MONSTER

The angler fish looks scary. It has a tiny, glowing light that hangs above its head. This attracts prey, which soon meet a bloody end in the angler's fanged jaws. This fish is only the size of a baby's fist. Hopefully, there are no bigger angler fish **lurking** down there.

The coelacanth is still out there. 〈〈

prey animal that is killed and eaten by another animal
species type or sort of living thing

HEAD FOUND IN SHARK

Fishermen had a shock in 2001 when they caught a tiger shark off Australia's east coast. When they cut open the 13-foot (4-meter) long shark, a human head rolled out. The police had a mystery on their hands. Whoever he was, the victim had probably drowned before the shark ate his head whole.

HUNTERS

We already know about 400 different types of sharks, but there could be many more living in the depths of the oceans. We still know very little about sharks.

SUPERFISH

Sharks are some of the oldest creatures on the earth. They first appeared 400 million years ago. (That is about 200 million years before dinosaurs.) They do not seem to get diseases like some fish, since they have a strong **immune** system.

Sharks do an important job. They are garbage collectors and get rid of ill or weak fish. They get a bad name from the few sharks that have hurt people. Most sharks are harmless to humans.

More people are killed each year by bee stings than by sharks.

WEIRD WORDS   immune protected against disease

MONSTERS

In the last few years, people have seen sharks in the Pacific Ocean that are even larger than great white sharks. They may grow to over 33 feet (10 meters) long. They live so far down that they are not likely to be a threat to humans.

BIG FISH

The biggest living fish is the whale shark. It can grow up to 50 feet (15 meters) long and can weigh more than 15 tons. It feeds on **plankton** and does not harm humans. It is thought to live for up to 150 years.

In 1918 fishermen in Australia reported seeing a huge shark take their crayfish traps. They said the monster of a shark was 115 feet (35 meters) long!

ONCE BITTEN, TWICE UNLUCKY!

A shark once had its own mystery to figure out. In 1968 Henry Bource was filming sharks off the coast of Australia, when one bit off his leg. Luckily for him, it took his false leg. He had worn it since he lost his real leg to another shark.

The whale shark is the world's largest fish.

There are only 50 to 75 reported shark attacks in the world each year.

plankton very tiny shrimplike organisms that float in the ocean

MEGALODON

Large teeth from the Megalodon shark have been found and dated at just 11,000 years old. That is not very long ago, compared to the millions of years the shark has been around. Is it possible that the Megalodon has **survived** to modern times?

LARGE KILLERS

There might be a monster twice the size of a great white shark deep in the oceans. Whether this huge creature still exists is a mystery. A great white shark is scary enough at 26 feet (8 meters) long. The film *Jaws* gave this powerful creature a bad name. Everyone saw it as a deadly human-eater. So what would they make of its **ancestor**?

MONSTER SHARK

Skeletons and jaws have been found that belong to a monster shark. It was called Megalodon. Although it may have been **extinct** for many years, some people believe these "eating machines" could still be out there. Scientists have yet to solve the mystery.

The film *Jaws* used a fake shark.

The size of its teeth show that the Megalodon was three times as big as a great white shark.

ancestor relative from the past
extinct died out, never to return

MEGAMOUTH

Can there really be large sharks we have not yet seen deep in the ocean? In 1976 the Unites States Navy caught a shark weighing more than a ton. No one had seen a creature like this before. They called it a megamouth. Since then, about twelve more have been found. Three fishermen caught one in the Philippines in 1998. The megamouth is very rare and does not harm humans. Like the gentle whale shark, its huge mouth is for sifting **plankton** from the sea.

The first female megamouth to be found was washed up on a beach in South Africa in 2002. She was about 13 feet (4 meters) long. Scientists were thrilled to find her—but still **mystified**.

The megamouth shark is harmless to humans, just like this basking shark. **‹‹**

mystified puzzled and baffled

GIANT FACTS AND FIGURES

The world's largest known sea creatures include:

Largest fish	Whale shark. Record of 66 ft (20 m) long.
Largest jellyfish	Over 6.6 ft (2 m) across the bell with a **tentacle** 130 ft (40 m) long.
Largest **carnivore**	Great white shark. Record of 30 ft (9 m) long, over 2.2 tons.

There may be bigger creatures out there that we have not yet found.

OCEAN GIANTS

Science fiction stories are full of giant sea creatures that attack any diver in sight. A giant crab may rip apart a human in a horror film, but can it happen in real life? The ocean's giants have always amazed us.

A giant spider crab's body can be 12 inches (30 centimeters) across. It can weigh 14 pounds (6.5 kilograms), with a leg span of 13 feet (4 meters). It may not eat you, but it could give you quite a bite.

There are huge clams in the South Pacific. They can grow up to 4 feet (1.2 meters) across. Although they have been given the name "man-eating clam," they shut too slowly to trap a diver.

A giant jellyfish off the coast of the U.S.

carnivore animal that eats other animals
science fiction made-up stories that twist the facts of science

THE TRUE GIANT

The blue whale is the largest mammal on Earth. It can reach 98 feet (30 meters) long. It can weigh more than 220 tons. Its heart is the size of a car. Blue whales feed on **plankton** and are harmless to humans. They are now rare and near **extinction** because they were once hunted for their oil. In 1931 over 29,000 were killed in one season.

One mystery of these magnificent creatures is how they communicate with each other across hundreds of miles of ocean. They seem to have their own language of rumbles and clicks. Whales are some of the most intelligent creatures on the planet.

The giant reef clam is beautifully colored.

EATEN ALIVE

In 1891 James Bartley was whaling off the Falkland Islands in the South Atlantic Ocean. He fell overboard and was swallowed by a sperm whale. Two days later the whale was caught and cut open. Bartley was in the whale's stomach, barely alive. His skin was bleached white. Somehow he recovered.

Blue whales must rise to the surface to breathe.

tentacle long arm of a squid or jellyfish

GIGANTIC

It is a mystery how a giant squid can grow so huge. The longest tentacles seen so far stretched to over 65 feet (20 meters). Could giant squid eat humans? It is possible. Some stories mention such attacks. We cannot go down to its home, deep in the ocean **trenches.** Will we ever know how huge these squid can get?

GIANT SQUID

Of all the creatures in the ocean, perhaps the most mysterious is the giant squid. We know so little about it. That is because none have been seen alive. They live very deep down, but sometimes they get washed up on beaches. Some are known to be longer than two buses.

ATTACK

In 1941 the Germans sank a British ship in the Atlantic. Suddenly a giant squid came to the surface. It wrapped a **tentacle** around one man and pulled him under. He was not seen again. Then a tentacle grabbed another man's leg. The suckers on its tentacles pulled his skin and left sores. He was rescued, but his legs were scarred for years.

The suckers of a giant squid are lined with razor-sharp teeth.

WEIRD WORDS   skipper person in charge of a boat

MONSTER SQUID GRIPS RACING YACHT

In 2003 a yacht in the Jules Verne around-the-world sailing competition met with mystery. The yacht was suddenly gripped by giant arms for over an hour in the mid-Atlantic.

"The giant squid was pulling really hard. I've been sailing for 40 years, and I've never seen anything like it," said the **skipper.**

One of the French crew saw the creature through a porthole. "The arms were as thick as mine in an oil-skin. I thought of the damage it could do. When we saw it behind the boat it must have been 30 feet (9 meters) long," he said. Many people thought the sailors must have been mistaken.

Giant squid have a parrotlike beak, eight arms, and two long tentacles to grab food.

20,000 LEAGUES UNDER THE SEA

Jules Verne was a writer of **science fiction.** In 1868 he wrote this famous story set under the ocean. A giant squid had a fight with a submarine. Captain Nemo and his *Nautilus* crew battled with the mystery monster.

FROM MYSTERY TO KNOWLEDGE

EARLY FINDS

Only since the 1800s have scientists discovered animals and plants living at great depths.

1818: Sir John Ross lowers a line half a mile (1 km) under the sea and finds worms and a starfish.

1843: Edward Forbes says no life can exist below 2,000 ft (600 m).

1872-1876: A ship lowers gear into the deep, finding hundreds of unknown animals.

Each year we discover new facts about ocean life. The oceans are slowly revealing some of their dark secrets.

People have only been able to go deep into the sea in the last 50 years. In 1960 a mini-submarine dived 6 miles (11 kilometers) down for the first time in history. Three years later it found an American submarine that had sunk, killing 129 men. It was found 1.2 miles (2 kilometers) down.

Deep-sea exploring solved more mysteries in the 1980s. American teams traveled several miles down in a submarine called *Alvin*. They saw **volcanic vents** that blew out clouds of black smoke and water hot enough to melt lead.

Modern submarines can reach great depths.

ALVIN

A robotic arm on a submarine was used to collect things from the *Titanic* wreck.

WEIRD WORDS   the bends sickness caused by coming up from a deep dive too quickly

EXPLORING BELOW

In 1988 treasure hunters dived down more than half a mile (one kilometer) near South Carolina. They found a wooden ship that had sunk in 1857. The ship was full of gold. Robert Ballard, the famous scientist and deep-sea diver, has found ancient ships deep in the Mediterranean. One was a Roman ship from the 4th century.

In 1993 Japan began work on Kaiko—the world's deepest-diving robot camera. Kaiko has since dived more than 6 miles (11 kilometers) down. Its pictures have shown that the eerie darkness is alive with small animals.

In 1997 a robot called *Odyssey* was used to look for giant squid in the dark water off New Zealand. The search for mysterious deep-sea creatures has only just begun.

THE BENDS

Divers years ago took great risks. When divers come up to the surface too fast, the change in pressure can form gas bubbles in their blood. Many got ill from this condition, called **the bends,** and some even died.

The bends used to be a real mystery for divers. Now they spend time in **decompression chambers** to avoid getting ill. >>

FACTS AND FIGURES

Can it really be true?

- Eighty percent of all life on the earth is found under the ocean.

- Ninety-seven percent of the earth's water is saltwater ocean.

- Eighty-five per cent of this water is the cold, deep sea 2.5 miles (3.8 kilometers) below the surface.

- Ninety percent of all **volcanic** activity occurs in the ocean.

MYSTERIES SOLVED

We are just on the brink of major discoveries. Who knows what we might find deep down in the ocean? We may find the enormous creatures that the sailors of long ago talked about.

The water pressure at deep depths is extreme. In the deepest parts of the ocean, it can be like 50 jumbo jets pushing down on one person. Yet tiny creatures live there that we have not even met yet.

We have not even discovered all the mysteries of the Great Barrier **Reef** in Australia. At 1,250 miles (2,000 kilometers) long, it is the largest living structure on Earth. It can even be seen from the moon.

Building under the sea has started already. This is an underwater hotel in Florida.

THE SEARCH GOES ON

The sea will always be a world of mystery. Even so, we will keep trying to solve many of its riddles. What will we discover in the next few years?

- Are the wrecks of missing planes and boats still out there?
- Are there clues to Atlantis and other lost worlds?
- What is the truth behind the Bermuda Triangle and its powers?
- How many new sea creatures will we discover?
- Will huge sea **serpents** be filmed for the first time?
- Will we save the oceans from over-fishing, pollution, and destruction?
- Will we live and work in underwater buildings ?

These are just some of the questions we hope to answer in the near future.

THE DEEP OF THE FUTURE

One of the big mysteries facing the future of our planet is how much deeper "the deep" will get. On average, the sea has risen 4–10 inches (10–25 centimeters) over the past 100 years. If the world's ice caps melt, the sea will rise another 217 feet (66 meters). We may have to live underwater ourselves one day. This could be the biggest mystery of the deep in the future.

What mysteries still **lurk** in the planet's great oceans? **《**

FIND OUT MORE

WEBSITES

SHARK TRUST
Information about sharks and their conservation.
sharktrust.org

BERMUDA TRIANGLE
History of the triangle and lists of all the boats and planes that were lost there.
bermudatriangle.org

MARINE BIO
Find out about the weirdest sea creatures on this large site.
marinebio.com

BOOKS
Martsen, Bradford. *The Incredible Hunt for the Giant Squid*. Berkeley Heights, New Jersey: Enslow, 2003.

Oxlade, C., and A. Ganeri. *The Mystery of the Bermuda Triangle*. Chicago: Heinemann, 1999.

Townsend, John. *Incredible Fish*. Chicago: Raintree, 2004.

Wallace, Holly. *The Mystery of Atlantis*. Chicago: Heinemann, 2002.

WORLD WIDE WEB
If you want to find out more about mysteries of the deep, you can search the Internet using keywords such as these:

- Bermuda Triangle
- megamouth shark
- coelacanth
- Titanic + wreck
- ocean + mysteries
- whirlpools
- giant squid

You can make your own keywords using headings or words from this book.

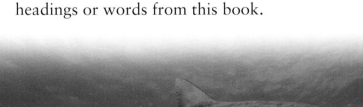

SEARCH TIPS

There are billions of pages on the Internet, so it can be difficult to find exactly what you are looking for. For example, if you just type in *water* on a search engine such as Google, you will get a list of 90 million web pages. These search skills will help you find useful websites more quickly:

- Use simple keywords, not whole sentences.
- Use two to six keywords in a search .
- Be precise—only use names of people, places, or things.
- If you want to find words that go together, put quote marks around them—for example, "giant squid" or "sea creatures."
- Use the advanced section of your search engine.
- Use the "+" sign to add certain words.

WHERE TO SEARCH

SEARCH ENGINE

A search engine looks through the entire web and lists all the sites that match the words in the search box. The best matches are at the top of the list, on the first page. Try searching with **google.com**.

SEARCH DIRECTORY

A search directory is like a library of websites. You can search by keyword or subject and browse through the different sites like you would look through books on a shelf. A good example is **yahooligans.com**.

GLOSSARY

adapt change or adjust

ancestor relative from the past

belch let out out gas noisily

capacity number of people that can fit onboard

carnivore animal that eats other animals

coincidence two or more seemingly connected strange things that happen at the same time

continent one of the earth's seven large land masses

coral hard undersea growth around tiny sea creatures

curse words that bring about supernatural powers and evil

decompression chamber room that brings a diver back to normal pressure very slowly

dread fear

Earth's crust layer of rock around the earth

erupt burst out suddenly

extinct died out, never to return

fate power thought to control what will happen

fleet large group of ships

flounder struggle

folklore old beliefs, myths, and stories

fossil ancient plant or animal remains that have been preserved as rock

funnel large metal chimney

glimpse take a quick look

Hindu belonging to the ancient Indian religion of Hinduism

hostile unfriendly or against you

Ice Age period of time when much of the earth was covered with ice

immune protected against disease

jinx unlucky force

landslide rapid falling of earth or rocks down a slope

lava hot liquid rock that flows from a volcano

legend story from long ago that may be partly true

logbook official diary of a ship's voyage

lurk wait around, ready to strike

maiden voyage first journey of a ship

mane long hair growing on the neck

mermaid make-believe sea creature with the body of a beautiful woman and the tail of a fish

meteorite large lump of rock, metal, or ice from outer space

mystified puzzled and baffled

myth made-up tale, told over time

New World North and South America

nuclear submarine submarine run by nuclear (atomic) power and carrying nuclear missiles

omen sign of good or evil

phantom ghostly appearance

plankton very tiny organisms that float in the sea

plaque stone or metal sign in memory of the dead

prey animal that is killed and eaten by another animal

psychic able to see the future and show unusual powers of the mind

reef ridge of rock or coral near the surface of the sea

retired taken from active service

rock formation natural feature made by the wearing away or movement of rock

science fiction made-up stories that may twist the facts of science

seabed bottom of the ocean

seaquake earthquake under the sea

serpent large snake

siren beautiful female creature in Greek myths whose singing attracted sailors. Those who followed the singing would meet a watery grave.

skipper person in charge of a boat

sonar using sound waves to detect objects underwater

spawn lay many eggs

species type or sort of living thing

stone tablets slabs of stone that are carved with writing

superstition belief based on faith in the supernatural

survive stay alive despite dangers

tentacle long arm of a squid or jellyfish

the bends sickness caused by coming up from a deep dive too quickly

tide daily rise and fall of the ocean

tornado violent, destructive whirling wind with a funnel cloud that moves in a narrow path over land

torpedo cigar-shaped underwater missile

trance sleeplike state

tremor shaking caused by an earthquake

trench deep ditch or valley

tsunami very large wave caused by an underwater earthquake

UFO Unidentified Flying Object

vent hole that lets out gas and smoke, like a chimney

Vikings Scandinavian sailors and pirates from the 8th to 11th century

volcano vent or opening in the earth's crust. Steam and melted rock (lava) flow from it.

volcanic having to do with volcanos

vortex mass of whirling fluid in a spiral

waterspout twisting column of water, like a tornado over the sea

whaling ship ship for hunting whales

whirlpool powerful circular current

INDEX